D1279779

POCKET POSITIVES

FOR OUR TIMES

POCKET POSITIVES

FOR OUR TIMES

Compiled by Maggie Pinkney

THE FIVE MILE PRESS

The Five Mile Press

The Five Mile Press Pty Ltd
950 Stud Road, Rowville
Victoria 3178 Australia
Phone: +61 3 8756 5500
Email: publishing@fivemile.com.au

First published 2002
Reprint 2003, 2004

All rights reserved

This compilation © The Five Mile Press Pty Ltd

Editor: Maggie Pinkney
Cover design: Zoë Murphy

Printed in China

National Library of Australia
Cataloguing-in-Publication data

Pocket positives for our times.

ISBN 1 86503 850 4

1. Quotations, English. 2. Optimism - Quotations, maxims,etc.
3. Success - Quotations, maxims, etc. I. Pinkney, Maggie.
082

Contents

INTRODUCTION

We have a choice about how we react to each new situation that arises – with hope or despair, with courage or fear, with enthusiasm or indifference. Now, more than ever before, it is great comfort to read the words of courageous men and women, the people who have walked the world stage – and made a difference. Such people as Nelson Mandela, Franklin D. Roosevelt, Winston Churchill, Aung San Suu Kyi and John F. Kennedy.

As British mathematician Jacob Bronowski points out, human beings have always feared for the future, and yet 'the emotional commitment of working together as one has made the Ascent of Man'.

Poets, novelists, religious leaders and philosophers have all had their say in this collection of quotations which are as different and varied as their authors. But all have one thing in common – they focus on life's positives and make light of the negatives.

Take heart from reading the collective wisdom of these wonderful minds!

HOLD ON
TO HOPE

Hope is the power
of being cheerful in circumstances
that we know to be desperate.

G. K. Chesterton, 1874–1936

ENGLISH WRITER, POET AND CRITIC

We should never let our fears

hold us back from

pursuing hopes.

———————

John F. Kennedy, 1917–1963

PRESIDENT OF THE UNITED STATES

The hope in the world
is still in dedicated minorities.
The trailblazers in human, academic,
scientific and religious freedom
have always been in the minority.

———————

Martin Luther King, 1929–1968

AMERICAN CIVIL RIGHTS LEADER AND MINISTER

$\mathcal{D}$o not fear to hope ... Each time

we smell the autumn's dying scent,

We know that primrose time

will come again.

Samuel Taylor Coleridge, 1772–1834

ENGLISH POET

$\mathcal{T}$rue hope is swift and flies

with swallow's wings;

Kings it makes gods,

and meaner creatures kings.

———————————

William Shakespeare, 1564–1616

There is one thing
which gives radiance to everything.
It is the idea of something
around the corner.

———————

G. K. Chesterton, 1874–1936

ENGLISH WRITER, POET AND CRITIC

T*here are no hopeless situations;*

there are only men who have

grown hopeless about them.

———————————

Clare Booth Luce, 1903–1987

AMERICAN PLAYWRIGHT

$\mathcal{H}$old your head high,

stick your chest out.

You can make it.

It gets dark sometimes

but morning comes ... Keep hope alive.

———————

Jesse Jackson, b. 1941

AMERICAN MINISTER, CIVIL RIGHTS LEADER AND CONGRESSMAN

Of all the forces

that make for a better world,

none is so indispensable,

none so powerful as hope.

Without hope man is only half alive.

———————

Charles Sawyer, 1887–1979

AMERICAN LAWYER

In *future days,*

which we seek to make more secure, we look forward to a world founded upon four essential freedoms. The first is the freedom of speech and expression — everywhere in the world. The second is freedom of every person to worship God in his own way — everywhere in the world. The third is freedom from want ... the fourth is freedom from fear.

Franklin D. Roosevelt, 1882–1945

PRESIDENT OF THE UNITED STATES OF AMERICA

$\mathcal{W}$e must accept finite disappointment,

but we must never lose infinite hope.

Martin Luther King, 1929–1968

AMERICAN CIVIL RIGHTS LEADER AND MINISTER

N*othing worth doing*

is completed in our lifetime;

therefore, we must be

saved by hope.

———————————

Reinhold Niebuhr, 1892–1971

AMERICAN THEOLOGIAN

For what human ill

does not dawn

seem to be an alleviation?

———————

Thornton Wilder, 1887–1975

AMERICAN WRITER

Everything that is done in the world is done by hope.

Martin Luther, 1483–1546

GERMAN RELIGIOUS REFORMER

$\mathcal{G}$reat hopes make great men.

Thomas Fuller, 1608–1661

ENGLISH CLERGYMAN AND HISTORIAN

MAKING IT HAPPEN

To will is to select a goal,

determine a course of action

that will bring one to that goal,

and then hold to that action

till the goal is reached.

The key is action.

———————

Michael Hansen, 1863–1908

AMERICAN MATHEMATICIAN

If you will it, it is no dream.

———————

Theodore Herzl, 1860–1904

ZIONIST FOUNDING FATHER

Just go out there and
do what you have to do.

———————

Martina Navratilova, b. 1956

CZECHOSLOVAKIAN-BORN AMERICAN TENNIS CHAMPION

*How wonderful it is
that nobody need wait a single
moment before starting to
improve the world.*

———————

Anne Frank, 1929–1945

GERMAN JEWISH SCHOOLGIRL DIARIST

Action may not
always bring happiness,
but there is no happiness
without action.

———————————————

Benjamin Disraeli, 1804–1881

ENGLISH STATESMAN AND WRITER

The first thing to do in life

is to do with purpose

what one proposes to do.

Pablo Casals, 1876–1973

SPANISH CELLIST, CONDUCTOR AND COMPOSER

The thing has already taken form in my mind before I start it. The first attempts are absolutely unbearable. I say this because I want you to know that if you see something worthwhile in what I am doing, it is not by accident but because of real direction and purpose.

———————

Vincent van Gogh, 1853–1890

DUTCH POST-IMPRESSIONIST PAINTER

If one advances confidently

in the direction of his dreams,

and endeavors to live the life

which he had imagined,

he will meet with a success

unexpected in common hours.

Henry David Thoreau, 1817–1862

AMERICAN ESSAYIST AND POET

S*ingleness of purpose*

is one of the chief essentials

for success in life,

no matter what may be

one's aim.

———————————

John D. Rockefeller, 1874–1960

AMERICAN OIL MILLIONAIRE AND PHILANTHROPIST

It's Up to You

If you think you're a winner you'll win,

If you dare to step out you'll succeed.

Believe in your heart, have a purpose to start,

Aim to help fellow man in his need.

Thoughts of faith must replace every doubt,

Words of courage and you cannot fail.

If you stumble and fall, rise and stand ten feet tall,

You determine the course that you sail.

———

Anonymous

Look at your life as a beautiful

fabric woven from wonderful

rich colours and fine cloth.

Make a plan, one that is full of

obtainable goals for a happy life.

Read through the plan daily so that

it becomes a permanent part

of your thought process.

———————

Sara Henderson, b. 1936

AUSTRALIAN OUTBACK STATION MANAGER AND WRITER

The man who does things
makes mistakes,
but he never makes the
biggest mistake of all –
doing nothing.

─────────────

Benjamin Franklin, 1706–1790

AMERICAN STATESMAN AND SCIENTIST

All things are possible
until they are proved impossible –
and even the impossible may only be so,
as of now.

———————————

Pearl S. Buck, 1892–1973

AMERICAN WRITER AND MISSIONARY

$\mathcal{I}f$ you don't like the way the world is,

you change it.

You have an obligation to change it.

You just do it one step at a time.

———————————

Marian Wright Edelman, b. 1937

AMERICAN ATTORNEY AND CIVIL RIGHTS ACTIVIST

Never look down to test the ground

before taking your next step;

only he who keeps his eye fixed on

the far horizon will find his right road.

———————

Dag Hammarskjold, 1905–1961

SWEDISH STATESMAN AND HUMANITARIAN

A
SPECIAL
KIND OF
COURAGE

$\mathscr{C}$ourage is the price life exacts

for granting peace.

———————————

Amelia Earhart, 1897–1937

AMERICAN AVIATOR

We are all afraid – for our confidence, for the future, for the world. That is the nature of the human imagination. Yet every man, every civilization, has gone forward because of its engagement with what it has set itself to do. The personal commitment and the emotional commitment of working together as one, has made the Ascent of Man.

———————————

Jacob Bronowski, 1908–1974

BRITISH MATHEMATICIAN, WRITER AND TV PRESENTER

Never give in!
Never give in!
Never, never, never, never —
in nothing great or small,
large or petty — never give in
except to convictions of
honor and good sense.

———————————

Winston Churchill, 1874–1965

BRITISH STATESMAN AND PRIME MINISTER

$\mathcal{M}$y personal trials have also taught me the value of unmerited suffering. As my sufferings mounted I soon realized that there were two ways that I could respond to my situation: either to react with bitterness or to transform the suffering into a creative force.

Martin Luther King, 1929–1968

AMERICAN CIVIL RIGHTS LEADER AND MINISTER

To endure is greater than to dare;

to tire out hostile fortune;

to be daunted by no difficulty;

to keep heart when all have lost it –

who can say this is not greatness?

———————————

William Makepeace Thackeray, 1811–1863

ENGLISH WRITER

Each time a man stands up for an ideal, or acts to improve the lot of others, or strikes out against injustice, he sends forth a tiny ripple of hope ... and crossing each other from a million different centers of energy and daring, those ripples build a current that can sweep down the mightiest walls of oppression and resistance.

———————————

Robert F. Kennedy, 1925–1967

AMERICAN LAWYER AND POLITICIAN

My message to you is:

Be courageous!

Be as brave as your fathers before you.

Have Faith!

Go forward.

———————————

Thomas Edison, 1847–1931

AMERICAN INVENTOR

If one advances confidently

in the direction of his dreams,

and endeavors to live the life

which he had imagined,

he will meet with a success

unexpected in common hours.

Henry David Thoreau, 1817–1862

AMERICAN ESSAYIST AND POET

Singleness of purpose

is one of the chief essentials

for success in life,

no matter what may be

one's aim.

———————————

John D. Rockefeller, 1874–1960

AMERICAN OIL MILLIONAIRE AND PHILANTHROPIST

$\mathcal{I}$t's Up to You

If you think you're a winner you'll win,

If you dare to step out you'll succeed.

Believe in your heart, have a purpose to start,

Aim to help fellow man in his need.

Thoughts of faith must replace every doubt,

Words of courage and you cannot fail.

If you stumble and fall, rise and stand ten feet tall,

You determine the course that you sail.

———

Anonymous

Look at your life as a beautiful

fabric woven from wonderful

rich colours and fine cloth.

Make a plan, one that is full of

obtainable goals for a happy life.

Read through the plan daily so that

it becomes a permanent part

of your thought process.

———————

Sara Henderson, b. 1936

AUSTRALIAN OUTBACK STATION MANAGER AND WRITER

The man who does things
makes mistakes,
but he never makes the
biggest mistake of all –
doing nothing.

———————

Benjamin Franklin, 1706–1790

AMERICAN STATESMAN AND SCIENTIST

All things are possible

until they are proved impossible –

and even the impossible may only be so,

as of now.

_____

Pearl S. Buck, 1892–1973

AMERICAN WRITER AND MISSIONARY

If you don't like the way the world is,

you change it.

You have an obligation to change it.

You just do it one step at a time.

———————————

Marian Wright Edelman, b. 1937

AMERICAN ATTORNEY AND CIVIL RIGHTS ACTIVIST

Never look down to test the ground

before taking your next step;

only he who keeps his eye fixed on

the far horizon will find his right road.

Dag Hammarskjold, 1905–1961

SWEDISH STATESMAN AND HUMANITARIAN

A

SPECIAL

KIND OF

COURAGE

Courage is the price life exacts

for granting peace.

Amelia Earhart, 1897–1937

AMERICAN AVIATOR

We are all afraid – for our confidence,
for the future, for the world. That is the nature
of the human imagination. Yet every man,
every civilization, has gone forward because of
its engagement with what it has set itself to do.
The personal commitment and the emotional
commitment of working together as one, has
made the Ascent of Man.

Jacob Bronowski, 1908–1974

BRITISH MATHEMATICIAN, WRITER AND TV PRESENTER

Never give in!

Never give in!

Never, never, never, never –

in nothing great or small,

large or petty – never give in

except to convictions of

honor and good sense.

———————————

Winston Churchill, 1874–1965

BRITISH STATESMAN AND PRIME MINISTER

My personal trials have also taught me the value of unmerited suffering. As my sufferings mounted I soon realized that there were two ways that I could respond to my situation: either to react with bitterness or to transform the suffering into a creative force.

———————

Martin Luther King, 1929–1968
AMERICAN CIVIL RIGHTS LEADER AND MINISTER

To endure is greater than to dare;

to tire out hostile fortune;

to be daunted by no difficulty;

to keep heart when all have lost it –

who can say this is not greatness?

William Makepeace Thackeray, 1811–1863

ENGLISH WRITER

Each time a man stands up for an ideal, or acts to improve the lot of others, or strikes out against injustice, he sends forth a tiny ripple of hope ... and crossing each other from a million different centers of energy and daring, those ripples build a current that can sweep down the mightiest walls of oppression and resistance.

Robert F. Kennedy, 1925–1967

AMERICAN LAWYER AND POLITICIAN

My message to you is:

Be courageous!

Be as brave as your fathers before you.

Have Faith!

Go forward.

———————————

Thomas Edison, 1847–1931

AMERICAN INVENTOR

$\mathcal{I}$ was raised to sense what someone else wanted me to be and to be that kind of person. It took me a long time not to judge myself through someone else's eyes.

———

Sally Field, b. 1946

AMERICAN ACTOR

$C$are no more for the opinions of others,

for those voices.

Do the hardest thing on earth for you.

Act for yourself.

Face the truth.

———————————

Katherine Mansfield, 1888–1923

NEW ZEALAND WRITER

I didn't belong as a kid,
and that always bothered me.
If only I'd known that one day
my differentness would be an asset,
then my early life would have been
much easier.

———————

Bette Midler, b. 1945

AMERICAN SINGER AND COMEDIAN

Our problem is that we make the mistake of comparing ourselves with other people. You are not inferior or superior to any human being ... You do not determine your success by comparing yourself to others, rather you determine your success by comparing your accomplishments to your capabilities. You are 'number one' when you do the best you can with what you have, every day.

———

Zig Siglar

AMERICAN MOTIVATIONAL WRITER

In everyone there is something precious,

found in no one else; so honor each man

for what is hidden within him –

for what he alone has,

and none of his fellows.

———————

Hasidic saying

*L*ow self-esteem

is like driving through life

with your handbrake on.

———————————

Maxwell Maltz, 1899–1975

AMERICAN SURGEON AND MOTIVATIONAL WRITER

I'm trying to be myself more and more.

The more confidence you have in yourself ...

the more you realize that this is you,

and life isn't long. So get on with it!

———————

Kylie Minogue, b. 1968

AUSTRALIAN SINGER AND ACTOR

Start treating yourself as if you're
the most important asset you'll ever have.

After all, aren't you?

———

Anonymous

You can do or be whatever you want in your own life.

Nothing can stop you, except for your own fears.

Don't blame anyone else ... you have the power to make the decision.

Just do it.

———————

Nola Diamatopoulos

AUSTRALIAN CREATIVE WORKSHOP TUTOR

My will shall shape the future. Whether I fail or succeed shall be no man's doing but my own. I am the force. I can clear any obstacle before me or I can be lost in the maze. My choice, my responsibility. Win or lose, only I hold the key to my destiny.

Elaine Maxwell

AMERICAN WRITER

THE Heart OF THE Matter

And now here is my secret,
a very simple secret; it is only with
the heart that one can see properly;
what is essential is invisible
to the eye.

Antoine de Saint-Exupéry, 1900–1944

FRENCH NOVELIST AND AVIATOR

To put the world in order we must first

put the nation in order.

To put the nation in order we must first

put the family in order.

To put the family in order we must first

cultivate our personal life.

And to cultivate our personal life,

we must set our hearts right.

Confucius, c. 550–478 BC

CHINESE PHILOSOPHER

T*he heart's affections are divided*

like the branches of the cedar tree; if the tree

loses one strong branch, it will suffer but it

does not die. It will pour all its vitality into

the next branch so that it will grow and fill

the empty space.

Kahlil Gibran, 1882–1931

LEBANESE POET, ARTIST AND MYSTIC

Love will teach us all things,

but we must learn how to win love. It is got

with difficulty: it is a possession dearly

bought with much labor and a long time,

for one must love not sometimes only but

always. And let not men's sin dishearten thee:

love a man even in his sin, for that love is a

likeness of the divine love, and is the summit

of love on earth.

Feodor Dostoevsky, 1821–1881

RUSSIAN NOVELIST

I love thee for a heart that's kind,

Not for the knowledge of thy mind.

―――――――――

W. H. Davies, 1871–1940

WELSH POET

All love is sweet,

Given or returned,

Common as light is love,

And its familiar voice

wearies not ever.

———————————

Percy Bysshe Shelley, 1792–1822

ENGLISH POET

A *loving heart is the truest wisdom.*

Charles Dickens, 1812–1870

ENGLISH NOVELIST

My heart is like a singing bird

Whose nest is in a watered shoot;

My heart is like an apple-tree

Whose boughs are bent with thickset fruit;

My heart is like a rainbow shell

That paddles in a halcyon sea;

My heart is gladder than all these

Because my love has come to me.

Christina Rosetti, 1830–1894

ENGLISH POET

If a good face is a letter of recommendation,

a good heart is a letter of credit.

———————————

Edward Bulwer-Lytton, 1803–1873

ENGLISH WRITER, DRAMATIST AND POET

Keep a green tree in your heart

and perhaps a singing bird

will come.

_____

Chinese proverb

$\mathcal{T}$he heart of the wise,

like a mirror,

should reflect all objects,

without being sullied by any.

———————

Confucius, c. 550–478 BC

CHINESE PHILOSOPHER

Learning to understand our dreams

is a matter of learning to understand

our heart's language.

———————

Anne Faraday, b. 1935,

AMERICAN PSYCHOLOGIST AND DREAM RESEARCHER

When thou prayest,

rather let thy heart be without words

than thy words without heart.

———————

John Bunyan, 1628–1688,

ENGLISH WRITER AND MORALIST

FAMILY TIES

My mother was the making of me.

She was so true, so sure of me, and I

felt that I had someone to live for;

someone I must not disappoint.

———————————

Thomas Edison, 1847–1931

AMERICAN INVENTOR

FROM A LETTER TO HER MOTHER

Whatever beauty or poetry is to be found in my little book is owing to your interest and encouragement of all my efforts from the first to the last; and if ever I do anything to be proud of, my greatest happiness will be that I can thank you for that, as I may do for all the good there is in me.

Louisa May Alcott, 1832–1888

AMERICAN NOVELIST

I'm doing this for my father.

I'm quite happy that they see me as

my father's daughter. My only concern

is that I prove worthy of him.

Aung San Suu Kyi, b. 1945

BURMA'S DEMOCRATICALLY ELECTED LEADER,
AND DAUGHTER OF BURMA'S HERO AUNG SAN

To bring up a child

in the way he should go,

travel that way yourself

once in a while.

———————————

Josh Billings, 1818–1885

AMERICAN HUMORIST

All that I am or hope to be,

I owe to my mother.

———————

Abraham Lincoln, 1809–1865

PRESIDENT OF THE UNITED STATES OF AMERICA

If a child lives with approval,

He learns to like himself.

———————

Dorothy Law Nolte

AMERICAN POET AND WRITER

By profession I am a soldier and take great pride in that fact, but I am prouder, infinitely prouder, to be a father. A soldier destroys in order to build; the father only builds, never destroys. The one has the potentialities of death; the other embodies creation and life. And while the hordes of death are mighty, the battalions of life are mightier still.

Douglas MacArthur, 1889–1964

AMERICAN MILITARY LEADER

There is no vocabulary

For the love within a family,

love that's lived in

But not looked at,

love within the light of which

All else is seen ...

T.S. Eliot, 1888–1965

AMERICAN-BORN BRITISH POET AND CRITIC

*C*hildren with the same family,

the same blood, with the same first

associations and habits, have some means

of enjoyment in their power, which no

subsequent connections can supply.

———————

Jane Austen, 1775–1816

ENGLISH NOVELIST

I long to put the experience of fifty years at once into your young lives, to give you at once the key of that treasure chamber every gem of which has cost me tears and struggles and prayers, but you must work for these inward treasures yourselves.

Harriet Beecher Stowe, 1811–1869

AMERICAN AUTHOR AND ABOLITIONIST

Your Children

You may strive to be like them but seek not

to make them like you.

For life goes not backward nor tarries

with yesterday.

You are the bows from which your children

as living arrows are sent forth.

The Archer sets the mark upon the path

of the infinite,

And He bends you with His might that

His arrows may go swift and far.

Let your bending in the Archer's hand

be for gladness;

For even as He loves the arrow that flies,

so he loves the bow that is stable.

———————

Kahlil Gibran, 1882–1931

LEBANESE POET, ARTIST AND MYSTIC

$\mathcal{F}$amily faces are magic mirrors.

Looking at people who belong to us,

we see the past, present and future.

———————

Gail Lumet Buckley, b. 1937

AMERICAN WRITER

At the end of your life,

you will never regret not having

passed one more test,

nor winning one more verdict or

not closing one more deal.

You will regret time not spent

with a husband, a friend,

a child or parent.

———————

Barbara Bush, b. 1925

FIRST LADY OF THE UNITED STATES OF AMERICA

$\mathcal{G}$od sent children for another purpose than merely to keep up the race – to enlarge our hearts; and to make us unselfish and full of kindly sympathies and affections; to give our souls higher aims; to call out all our faculties to extended enterprise and exertion; and to bring around our firesides bright faces, happy smiles and loving, tender hearts.

———————

Mary Botham Howitt, 1799–1888

ENGLISH AUTHOR

My mother had a great deal of trouble

with me, but I think she enjoyed it.

———————————

Mark Twain, 1835–1910

AMERICAN WRITER

I want my daughters to be beautiful,

accomplished, and good;

to be admired, loved and respected;

to have a happy youth,

to be well and wisely married,

and to lead useful, pleasant lives,

with as little care and sorrow to

try them as God sees fit to send.

Louisa May Alcott, 1832–1888

AMERICAN NOVELIST

There is no greater reward for a well-spent life than to see one's children well-started in life, owing to their parents' good health, good principles, fixed character, good breeding, and in general the whole outfit, that enables them to fight the battle of life with success.

William Graham Sumner, 1840–1910

AMERICAN SOCIOLOGIST

Love children especially for,

like angels, they too are sinless

and they live to soften and purify

our hearts and, as it were,

to guide us.

Feodor Dostoevsky, 1821–1881

RUSSIAN WRITER

And so our mothers and grandmothers have,

more often than not anonymously, handed on

the creative spark, the seed of the flower they

themselves never hoped to see – or like a sealed

letter they could not plainly read.

———————

Alice Walker, b. 1944

AMERICAN WRITER

I think it must be written somewhere
that the virtues of the mother
will be visited on the children.

_____

Charles Dickens, 1812–1870

ENGLISH NOVELIST

Home, Sweet Home

Home is any four walls

that enclose the right person.

Helen Rowland, 1875–1950

AMERICAN WRITER

$\mathcal{H}e$ *is happiest,*

be he king or peasant,

who finds peace in his home.

———————————

Johann von Goethe, 1749–1832

GERMAN WRITER, DRAMATIST AND SCIENTIST

$\mathcal{T}$he ornament of the house is

the friends who frequent it.

———————————

Ralph Waldo Emerson, 1803–1882

AMERICAN ESSAYIST, POET AND PHILOSOPHER

A man travels the world over
in search of what he needs and
returns home to find it.

———————

George Moore, 1852–1933
IRISH WRITER AND ART CRITIC

The ideal of happiness has always

taken material form in the house

whether cottage or castle;

it stands for permanence and

separation from the world.

———————

Simone de Beauvoir, 1908–1986

FRENCH NOVELIST

No place is more delightful

than one's own fireside.

———————

Cicero, 106–43 BC

ROMAN ORATOR, STATESMAN AND WRITER

$\mathcal{S}$eek home for rest,

For home is best.

Thomas Tusser, 1524–1580

ENGLISH FARMER

Few things, including clothes,

are more personal than your cherished ornaments.

The pioneer women, who crossed a wild continent

clutching their treasures to them, knew that a clock,

a picture, a pair of candlesticks, meant home,

even in the wilderness.

Good Housekeeping, *August 1952*

$\mathcal{I}f$ you want one golden rule that
will fit everybody, this is it.
Have nothing in your houses that
you do not know to be useful
or believe to be beautiful.

William Morris, 1834–1896

ENGLISH DESIGNER AND CRAFTSMAN

B*ut what on earth*

is half so dear – so longed for –

as the hearth of home?

———————

Emily Brontë, 1818–1848

ENGLISH POET AND NOVELIST

*W*hom God loves,

his house is sweet to him.

———————

Miguel de Cervantes, 1547–1616

SPANISH WRITE

A *comfortable home is*

a great source of happiness.

It ranks immediately after health

and a good conscience.

———————

Sydney Smith, 1771–1843

ENGLISH ESSAYIST, CLERGYMAN AND WRITER

My kitchen is a mystical place,

a kind of temple for me. It is a place

where the sounds and odors carry

meaning that transfers from the past

and bridges to the future.

———————

Pearl Bailey, 1918–1986

AMERICAN SINGER

T*he strength of a nation is derived*

from the integrity of its homes.

———————

Confucius, c. 551–478 BC

CHINESE PHILOSOPHER

$\mathcal{M}$id pleasures and palaces

we may roam,

Be it ever so humble,

there's no place like home.

———————

J. H. Payne, 1791–1852

AMERICAN DRAMATIST, POET AND ACTOR

Thank Heavens for Friends

T*rue happiness consists not in the multitude of friends, but in the worth and choice.*

_____

Ben Jonson, c.1573–1637

ENGLISH DRAMATIST AND POET

You can always tell a real friend:

when you've made a fool

of yourself he doesn't feel

you've done a

permanent job.

Laurence J. Peter, b. 1918

CANADIAN WRITER

T*he antidote for fifty enemies*

is one friend.

Aristotle, 384–322 BC

GREEK PHILOSOPHER

$\mathcal{T}$rue friendship is a plant of slow growth

and must undergo and withstand

the shocks of adversity before it is

entitled to the appellation.

———————————

George Washington, 1732–1799

PRESIDENT OF THE UNITED STATES OF AMERICA

I *always felt that the great high privilege,*

relief and comfort of friendship was that

one had to explain nothing.

———————————

Katherine Mansfield, 1888–1923

NEW ZEALAND WRITER

Love is like the wild rose-briar;

Friendship like the holly tree.

The holly is dark when the rose-briar blooms,

But which one blooms most constantly?

———————

Emily Brontë, 1818–1848

ENGLISH NOVELIST AND POET

T*he better part of one's life*

consists of one's friendships.

———————————

Abraham Lincoln, 1809–1865

PRESIDENT OF THE UNITED STATES OF AMERICA

I have learned that to have a good friend

is the purest of all God's gifts,

for it is a love that has no exchange

or payment.

———————————

Frances Farmer, 1910–1970

AMERICAN ACTRESS AND WRITER

The proper office of a friend is to side with you when you are in the wrong. Nearly anybody will side with you when you are in the right.

Mark Twain, 1835–1910

AMERICAN WRITER

$\mathcal{I}$t is one of the blessings of friends

that you can afford to be

stupid with them.

Ralph Waldo Emerson, 1803–1882

AMERICAN ESSAYIST AND PHILOSOPHER

You can make more friends in two months by becoming interested in other people than you can in two years by trying to get other people interested in you.

Dale Carnegie, 1888–1955

AMERICAN MOTIVATIONAL WRITER

$\mathcal{T}$he world is a looking-glass,

and gives back to every man the

reflection of his own face.

———————————

William Makepeace Thackeray, 1811–1863

BRITISH WRITER

$\mathcal{T}$he only way

to have a friend

is to be one.

———————————

Ralph Waldo Emerson, 1803–1882

AMERICAN ESSAYIST AND PHILOSOPHER

F*ate chooses your relations,*

you choose your friends.

———————————

Jacques Delille, 1738–1813

FRENCH CLERIC AND POET

Friendship with oneself is all-important because without it one cannot be friends with anyone else in the world.

———————————

Eleanor Roosevelt, 1884–1962

FIRST LADY OF THE UNITED STATES OF AMERICA

$\mathcal{F}$riendship consists in forgetting

what one gives, and remembering

what one receives.

———————————

Alexandre Dumas, 1803–1870

FRENCH NOVELIST

I*f you want people to be glad to meet you,*

you must be glad to meet them –

and show it.

———————————

Johann von Goethe, 1749–1832

GERMAN POET, WRITER AND SCIENTIST

Friendship improves happiness and abates misery by doubling our joy and dividing our grief.

Joseph Addison, 1672–1719

ENGLISH ESSAYIST

It is fit for serene days,

and graceful gifts and country rambles, but

also for rough roads and hard fare, shipwreck,

poverty and persecution ... It should never

fall into something usual and settled, but add

rhyme and reason to what was drudgery.

Ralph Waldo Emerson, 1803–1882

AMERICAN ESSAYIST AND PHILOSOPHER

$\mathcal{I}$t is a good thing to be rich,

and a good thing to be strong,

but it is a better thing to be

loved by many friends.

———————

Euripides, c. 485–406 BC

GREEK DRAMATIST AND POET

𝒥riendship is the only cement

that will ever hold the world together.

———————————

Woodrow Wilson, 1856–1924

PRESIDENT OF THE UNITED STATES OF AMERICA

How to be Happy

I suspect that the happiest people you know are the ones who work at being kind, helpful and reliable – and happiness sneaks into their lives while they are busy doing those things. It is a by-product, never a primary goal.

———————

Harold S. Kushner

AMERICAN RABBI

There are as many nights as days,

and the one is just as long as the other in

the year's course. Even a happy life cannot

be without a measure of darkness, and

the word 'happy' would lose its meaning

if it were not balanced by sadness.

———————

Carl Jung, 1875–1961

SWISS PSYCHIATRIST

He who wishes to secure

the good of others has already

secured his own.

Confucius, c. 550–478 BC

CHINESE PHILOSOPHER

The secret of happiness is this:

let your interests be as wide as possible,

and let your reactions to the things

and persons that interest you be

as far as possible friendly

rather than hostile.

———————————

Bertrand Russell, 1872–1970

ENGLISH PHILOSOPHER, MATHEMATICIAN AND SOCIAL REFORMER

Youth is happy because it has the ability to see beauty. Anyone who keeps the ability to see beauty never grows old.

Franz Kafka, 1883–1924

CZECHOSLOVAKIAN-BORN GERMAN-SPEAKING WRITER

$\mathcal{I}$ hope never to feel completely fulfilled because then the point of the journey would be destroyed.
You have got to have curiosity, hunger and slight anxiety.

———————

Joanna Trollope, b. 1943

ENGLISH NOVELIST

Human felicity is produced not so much by great pieces of good fortune that seldom happen as by little advantages that occur every day.

———————————

Benjamin Franklin, 1706–1790

AMERICAN STATESMAN, SCIENTIST AND WRITER

$\mathcal{T}$here is a land of the living

and a land of the dead,

and the bridge is love.

———————————

Thornton Wilder, 1897–1975

AMERICAN DRAMATIST AND WRITER

A loving person lives in a loving world.

A hostile person lives in a hostile world.

Everyone you meet is your mirror.

—————

Ken Keyes Jr, 1921–1995

PERSONAL GROWTH LEADER AND PEACE ADVOCATE

Just don't give up trying to do

what you really want to do.

When there is love and inspiration,

I don't think you can go far wrong.

———————————

Ella Fitzgerald, 1918–1996

AMERICAN SINGER

Live as if everything you do

will eventually be known.

———————

Hugh Prather, b. 1938

AMERICAN WRITER

In spite of illness, in spite even of the arch-enemy sorrow, one can remain alive long past the usual date of disintegration if one is unafraid of change, insatiable in intellectual curiosity, interested in big things, and happy in small ways.

———

Edith Wharton, 1862–1937

AMERICAN NOVELIST

I accept life unconditionally.

Most people ask for happiness on condition.

Happiness can only be felt if

you don't set any condition.

———————

Artur Rubinstein, 1887–1982

POLISH-BORN PIANIST

$\mathcal{T}$o find out what one is fitted to do

and to secure an opportunity to do it

is the key to happiness.

———————

John Dewey, 1859–1952

AMERICAN EDUCATIONALIST, PHILOSOPHER AND REFORMER

$\mathcal{W}$*hat can be added to the happiness of*

a man who is in health, out of debt,

and has a clear conscience?

———————

Adam Smith, 1723–1790

SCOTTISH ECONOMIST, PHILOSOPHER AND ESSAYIST

GETTING IN TOUCH WITH YOUR CREATIVITY

Creativity is so delicate a flower

that praise tends to make it bloom,

while discouragement often nips it in the bud.

Any of us will put out more and better ideas

if our efforts are appreciated.

———————

Alex F. Osborn, 1888–1966

AMERICAN ADVERTISING DIRECTOR

When I am ... completely myself,

entirely alone ... or during the night when

I cannot sleep, it is on such occasions that

my ideas flow best and most abundantly.

When and how these come I know not,

nor can I force them.

Wolfgang Amadeus Mozart, 1756–1791

AUSTRIAN MUSICIAN AND COMPOSER

$\mathcal{G}$o cherish your soul;

expel companions;

set your habits to a life of solitude;

then will the faculties rise

fair and full within.

Ralph Waldo Emerson, 1803–1882

AMERICAN ESSAYIST AND POET

*E*mptiness is a symptom

that you are not living creatively.

You either have no goal that is

important enough to you, or you are

not using your talents and efforts

in striving toward an important goal.

———————

Maxwell Maltz, 1899–1975

AMERICAN SURGEON AND MOTIVATIONAL WRITER

$\mathcal{T}$o me, the difference between

the artist and the non-artist

is that the artist is

the one that does it.

———————

Helen Garner, b. 1945

AUSTRALIAN WRITER

A great many people who come
to creative writing classes intend
to write books 'one day'.
A book has to be written all the time,
it will not write itself one day.
A sense of dedication is necessary
to the writer.

Elizabeth Jolley, b. 1923

AUSTRALIAN WRITER

Don't think!

Thinking is the enemy of creativity.

It's self-conscious,

and anything self-conscious is lousy.

You can't try to do things;

you simply must do them.

Ray Bradbury, b. 1920

AMERICAN SCIENCE FICTION WRITER

When in doubt, make a fool of yourself.

There is a microscopically thin line between

being brilliantly creative and acting like

the most gigantic idiot on earth.

So what the hell, leap!

———————

Cynthia Heimel

AMERICAN WRITER

No *matter how old you get,*

if you can keep the desire to be creative,

you're keeping the man-child alive.

———————————

John Cassevetes, 1929–1989

AMERICAN FILM DIRECTOR

What is originality?

It is being one's self, and

reporting accurately what we see.

———————————————

Ralph Waldo Emerson, 1803–1882

AMERICAN ESSAYIST AND POET

All *you have to do*

is close your eyes and

wait for the symbols.

———————————

Tennessee Williams, 1911–1983

AMERICAN DRAMATIST AND WRITER

From Nine to Five

T*he best careers advice to the young is:*

'Find out what you like doing best and

get someone to pay you for doing it'.

Katharine Whitehorn, b. 1926

ENGLISH NEWSPAPER COLUMNIST

Never turn down a job

because you think it's too small;

you don't know where it could lead.

———————————

Julia Morgan, 1872–1957

AMERICAN ARCHITECT

I think we have to appreciate that we're alive for only a limited period of time, and we'll spend most of our lives working. That being the case, I believe one of the most important priorities is to do whatever we do as well as we can. We should take pride in that.

Victor Kermit Kiam, b. 1926

AMERICAN CORPORATE EXECUTIVE

$\mathcal{I}$n order that people

may be happy in their work,

these three things are needed.

They must be fit for it.

They must not do too much of it.

And they must have a sense of success in it.

John Ruskin, 1819–1900

ENGLISH ART CRITIC, PHILOSOPHER AND REFORMER

$\mathcal{W}$ork is the grand cure

of all the maladies and miseries

that ever beset man.

———————————

Thomas Carlyle, 1795–1881

SCOTTISH HISTORIAN AND ESSAYIST

No man deserves sympathy

because he has to work ... Far and away

the best prize that life offers is the chance

to work hard at work worth doing.

———————

Theodore Roosevelt, 1858–1919

PRESIDENT OF THE UNITED STATES OF AMERICA

$\mathcal{E}$ach morning sees some task begun,

Each evening sees its close.

Something attempted, something done,

Has earned a night's repose.

Henry Wadsworth Longfellow, 1807–1882

AMERICAN POET

*T*hank *G*od –

every morning when you get up – that you

have something to do which must be done,

whether you like it or not. Being forced to

work, and forced to do your best, will breed

in you a hundred virtues which the idle will

never know.

Charles Kingsley, 1819–1875

ENGLISH WRITER, POET AND CLERGYMAN

*W*ho said you should be happy?

Do your work.

———————

Colette, 1873–1954

FRENCH WRITER

$\mathcal{I}$t is impossible

to enjoy idling thoroughly

unless one has

plenty of work to do.

———————————

Jerome K. Jerome, 1859–1927

ENGLISH PLAYWRIGHT AND HUMORIST

The highest reward for man's toil

is not what he gets out of it

but what he becomes by it.

———————

John Ruskin, 1819–1900

ENGLISH ART CRITIC, PHILOSOPHER AND REFORMER

To my mind,

the best investment a young man

starting out in business could possibly make

is to give all his time, all his energies,

to work – just plain hard work.

Charles M. Schwab, 1862–1939

AMERICAN INDUSTRIALIST

The glory of a workman,

still more of a master-workman,

that he does his work well,

ought to be his most precious possession;

like the 'honor of a soldier',

dearer to him than life.

———————

Thomas Carlyle, 1795–1881

SCOTTISH HISTORIAN AND ESSAYIST

$\mathcal{T}$he force, the mass of character, mind, heart

or soul that a man can put into any work,

is the most important factor in that work.

A.P. Peabody, 1811–1893

AMERICAN WRITER

It is work that gives flavor to life.

Henri Frederic Amiel, 1828–1881

GETTING AHEAD

*O*ften the difference between

a successful person and a failure

is not that one has better abilities or ideas,

but the courage one has to bet on one's ideas,

to take a calculated risk – and to act.

Maxwell Maltz, 1899–1975

AMERICAN SURGEON AND MOTIVATIONAL WRITER

$\mathcal{F}$ew people think more than

two or three times a year.

I have made an international reputation

for myself by thinking once

or twice a week.

———————————

George Bernard Shaw, 1856–1950

IRISH DRAMATIST, WRITER AND CRITIC

Laziness may appear attractive,

but work gives satisfaction.

———————————

Anne Frank, 1929–1945

JEWISH SCHOOLGIRL DIARIST

To love what you do

and feel that it matters –

how could anything

be more fun?

———————

Katherine Graham, b. 1918

AMERICAN NEWSPAPER PUBLISHER

Believe in the best, think your best, study your best, have a goal for the best, never be satisfied with less than your best, try your best, and in the long run things will turn out for the best.

———————

Henry Ford, 1863–1947

AMERICAN CAR MANUFACTURER

$\mathcal{D}$o one more thing

at the end of the day and at the

end of the year you'll have done

365 more things.

———————

Richard Pratt

AUSTRALIAN PACKAGING MILLIONAIRE

A*chievement is largely the product of steadily raising one's level of aspiration and expectation.*

———————

Jack Nicklaus, b. 1940

AMERICAN GOLFER

All successful people have a goal.
No one can get anywhere unless he
knows where he wants to go and
what he wants to do or be.

————————

Norman Vincent Peale, 1898–1993

AMERICAN WRITER AND MINISTER

Do your work with all your heart

and you will succeed –

there's so little competition.

———————————

Elbert Hubbard, 1856–1915

AMERICAN WRITER

People who are unable to motivate themselves must be content with mediocrity, no matter how impressive their other talents.

———————

Andrew Carnegie, 1835–1919

SCOTTISH-BORN AMERICAN INDUSTRIALIST
AND PHILANTHROPIST

T*he secret of success is to do the*

common things uncommonly well.

———————————

John D. Rockefeller, 1839–1937

AMERICAN OIL MILLIONAIRE AND PHILANTHROPIST

*What is opportunity,
and when does it knock? It never knocks.
You can wait a whole lifetime, listening and
hoping, and you will hear no knocking. None
at all. You are opportunity, and you must
knock on the door leading to your destiny. You
prepare yourself to recognize opportunity, to
pursue and seize opportunity as you develop
the strength of your personality, and build a
self-image with which you are able to live.*

Maxwell Maltz, 1899–1975

AMERICAN SURGEON AND MOTIVATIONAL WRITER

Success is to be measured not so much by the position one has reached in life, as by the obstacles which one has overcome while trying to succeed.

———————

Booker Washington, 1856–1915

AMERICAN TEACHER, WRITER AND SPEAKER

One person's definition of success

is another's first step.

Only you can rate your accomplishments,

and find peace within yourself.

———

Anonymous

It's adding the 'extra'

to the ordinary —

and that takes persistence.

Bryce Courtenay, b. 1933

AUSTRALIAN BEST-SELLING AUTHOR

One Faith

'*I*' and 'you' are but the lattices,

In the niches of a lamp,

Through which the One Light shines.

'*I*' and 'you' are the veil

Between heaven and earth;

Lift this veil and you will see

No longer the bond of sects and creeds.

When 'I' and 'you' do not exist,

What is mosque, what is synagogue?

What is the Temple of Fire?

———————————

Sa'd al-din Mahmud Shabistari, c. 1250–1320

THE SECRET ROSE GARDEN

*H*urt not others with that
which pains yourself.

———————

Buddhist wisdom

Do unto others

as you would have them

do unto you.

———————

Jesus of Nazareth

$\mathcal{D}$o unto all men

as you would wish

to have done unto you;

and reject for others

what you would reject

for yourself.

———————

Islamic wisdom

This is the sum of all true righteousness –

Treat others, as thou wouldst thyself be treated.

Do nothing to thy neighbor, which hereafter

Thou wouldst not have thy neighbor do to thee.

———————

Hindu wisdom

Seek to be in harmony with all

your neighbors;

live in amity with your brethren.

————————————

Confucius, c. 550– 478 BC

CHINESE PHILOSOPHER

$\mathcal{T}$he West is not higher than the East,

nor is the West lower than the East,

and the difference that stands between

the two is not greater than the difference

between the tiger and the lion.

———————

Kahlil Gibran, 1882–1931

LEBANESE POET, ARTIST AND MYSTIC

$\mathcal{S}$hall I tell you what acts

are better than fasting, charity and prayers?

Making peace between enemies are such acts;

for enmity and malice tear up

the heavenly rewards by the roots.

———

The Koran

I *love you my brother,*

whoever you are – whether you worship in your

church, kneel in your temple, or pray in your

mosque. You and I are all children of one faith,

for the divers paths of religion are fingers of

the one loving hand of one Supreme Being,

a hand extended to all, offering completeness

of spirit to all, eager to receive all.

———————

Kahlil Gibran, 1882–1931

LEBANESE POET, ARTIST AND MYSTIC

All creatures are the family of God;

and he is the most beloved of God

who does most good unto His family.

———————

Islamic wisdom

The whole of mankind

belongs to one religion,

The religion of man.

For all men

God is the Father.

As the children of one God,

All men are brothers.

———

Sai Baba

INDIAN SPIRITUAL MASTER

If you have abandoned one faith,

do not abandon all faith.

There is always an alternative

to the faith we lose.

Or could it be the same thing

under another mask?

Graham Greene, 1904–1991

ENGLISH NOVELIST

WHAT'S IT ALL ABOUT?

The ideals that have lighted my way and, time after time, have given me new courage to face life cheerfully have been Kindness, Beauty and Truth.

Albert Einstein, 1879–1955

GERMAN-BORN AMERICAN PHYSICIST

Be a good human being,

a warm-hearted affectionate person. That is

my fundamental belief. Having a sense of

caring, a feeling of compassion will bring

happiness or peace of mind to oneself and

automatically create a positive atmosphere.

Dalai Lama, b. 1935

TIBETAN SPIRITUAL LEADER

Life is not made up of

great sacrifices and duties

but of little things

in which smiles and kindness

given habitually are what

win and preserve the heart

and secure comfort.

———————————

Sir Humphrey Davy, 1778–1829

ENGLISH CHEMIST AND INVENTOR

The only interest in living

comes from believing in life,

from loving life and using all the

power of your intelligence

to know it better.

———————————

Emile Zola, 1840–1902

FRENCH WRITER

What is the use of living if not to strive for noble causes and to make this muddled world a better place for those who will live in it after we are gone.

———————

Winston Churchill, 1874–1965

BRITISH PRIME MINISTER

$\mathcal{L}$ife was meant to be lived.

Curiosity must be kept alive.

One must never, for whatever reason,

turn his back on life.

———————

Eleanor Roosevelt, 1884–1962

FIRST LADY OF THE UNITED STATES OF AMERICA

W hat do we live for,

if it is not to make life less difficult

for each other.

_____

George Eliot, 1819–1880

ENGLISH NOVELIST

The root of the matter is a very simple old-fashioned thing, a thing so simple that I am almost ashamed to mention it for fear of the derisive smile with which wise cynics will greet my words. The thing I mean – please forgive me for mentioning it – is love, or compassion. If you feel this, you have a motive for existence, a guide to action, a reason for courage, an imperative necessity for intellectual honesty.

Bertrand Russell, 1872–1970

ENGLISH PHILOSOPHER, MATHEMATICIAN AND SOCIAL REFORMER

The great essentials to happiness in this life are something to do, something to love and something to hope for.

Joseph Addison, 1672–1719

ENGLISH ESSAYIST

Who will tell whether

one happy moment of love, or the joy of

breathing or walking on a bright morning and

smelling the fresh air, is not worth all the

suffering and effort that life implies?

Eric Fromm, 1900–1980

AMERICAN PSYCHOANALYST

B*elieve that life is worth living,*

and your belief will help create the fact.

——————————

William James, 1842–1910

AMERICAN PSYCHOLOGIST AND PHILOSOPHER

Getting money

is not all a man's business;

to cultivate kindness is

a valuable part of the

business of life.

———————————

Dr Samuel Johnson, 1709–1784

ENGLISH LEXICOGRAPHER, CRITIC AND WRITER

I expect to pass through life but once.

If, therefore, there be

any kindness I can show,

or any good thing I can do

to any fellow being,

let me do it now,

for I shall not pass

this way again.

William Penn, 1644–1718

ENGLISH QUAKER AND FOUNDER OF PENNSYLVANIA, USA

PEACE

ON EARTH...

$\mathcal{Y}$ou may either win your peace or buy it;

win it, by resisting evil; or buy it,

by compromising with evil.

———————

John Ruskin, 1819–1900

ENGLISH ART CRITIC, PHILOSOPHER AND ESSAYIST

Since wars begin in the minds of men,

it is in the minds of men that the

defenses of peace must be constructed.

———————

Constitution of UNESCO

$\mathcal{P}$eace cannot be kept by force.

It can only be achieved

by understanding.

————————————

Albert Einstein, 1879–1955

GERMAN-BORN AMERICAN PHYSICIST

Mankind has become so much one family that we cannot ensure our own prosperity except by insuring that of everyone else. If you wish to be happy yourself, you must resign yourself to seeing others also happy ...

———————

Bertrand Russell, 1872–1970

ENGLISH PHILOSOPHER, MATHEMATICIAN AND SOCIAL REFORMER

Anyone can forge a little link of brotherhood, or at least understanding. Some day perhaps every boy and girl will have become at home in a foreign country, and there could be no more useful step towards the abolition of war.

Havelock Ellis, 1859–1939

ENGLISH SEXOLOGIST AND ESSAYIST

Our strength lies,

not in our proving grounds and our

stockpiles, but in our ideals, our goals

and their universal appeal to all men

who are struggling to breathe free.

———————————

Adlai Stevenson, 1900–1965

AMERICAN STATESMAN AND UN REPRESENTATIVE

Not until the creation and maintenance of decent conditions of life for all men are recognized and accepted as a common obligation of all men ... shall we ... be able to speak of mankind as civilized.

Albert Einstein, 1879–1955

GERMAN-BORN AMERICAN PHYSICIST

Let there be justice for all.

Let there be peace for all.

Let there be work, bread, water and salt for all.

Let each know that for each the body,

mind and soul have been freed

to fulfill themselves.

———————

Nelson Mandela, b. 1918

PRESIDENT OF SOUTH AFRICA

$\mathcal{T}$he religion of non-violence is not meant

merely for the rishis and saints.

It is meant for the common people as well.

Non-violence is the law of our species,

as violence is the law of the brute.

———————————

Mahatma Gandhi, 1869–1948

INDIAN POLITICAL LEADER

All your strength is in your union,

All your danger is in discord,

Therefore be at peace henceforward,

And like brothers live together.

———————————

Henry Wadsworth Longfellow, 1807–1882

AMERICAN POET

T _oday we are faced with the pre-eminent fact_

that if civilization is to survive, we must

cultivate the science of human relationships,

the ability of peoples of all kinds to live together

and to work together in the same world at peace.

———————————

Franklin D. Roosevelt, 1882–1945

PRESIDENT OF THE UNITED STATES OF AMERICA

We all live with the objective

of being happy;

our lives are all different

and yet the same.

———————

Anne Frank, 1929–1945

GERMAN JEWISH SCHOOLGIRL DIARIST

I*t must be a peace without victory —*

only a peace between equals can last.

———————————

Woodrow Wilson, 1856–1924

PRESIDENT OF THE UNITED STATES OF AMERICA

I am a man of peace. I believe in peace. But I do not want peace at any price. I do not want the peace that you find in stone; I do not want the peace that you find in the grave: but I do want the peace which you find embedded in the human breast, which is exposed to the arrows of the whole world, but which is protected from all harm by the power of Almighty God.

———————————

Mahatma Gandhi, 1869–1948
INDIAN POLITICAL LEADER

Let us never negotiate out of fear,

but let us never fear to negotiate.

———————

John F. Kennedy, 1917–1963

PRESIDENT OF THE UNITED STATES OF AMERICA

The peace we seek, founded upon decent trust and co-operative effort among nations, can be fortified not by weapons of war but by wheat and by cotton, by milk and by wool, by meat and by timber and by rice. These are words that translate into every language.

Dwight D. Eisenhower, 1890–1969

PRESIDENT OF THE UNITED STATES OF AMERICA

I do not want the peace

which passeth understanding,

I want the understanding

which bringeth peace.

———————

Helen Keller, 1880–1968

AMERICAN WRITER AND SCHOLAR

Lord, make me an instrument of your peace:

Where there is hatred, let me sow love,

Where there is injustice, pardon,

Where there is doubt, faith,

Where there is despair, hope,

Where there is dark, light,

Where there is sadness, joy.

St Francis of Assissi, 1181–1226

The world will never have lasting peace

so long as men reserve for war

the finest human qualities.

Peace, no less than war, requires idealism

and self-sacrifice and a righteous

and dynamic faith.

———————

John Foster Dulles, 1888–1959

AMERICAN SECRETARY OF STATE

Peace is a daily,

a weekly, a monthly process,

gradually changing opinions,

slowly eroding old barriers,

quietly building new structures.

And however undramatic

the pursuit of peace,

the pursuit must go on.

———————

John F. Kennedy, 1917–1963

PRESIDENT OF THE UNITED STATES OF AMERICA

$\mathcal{O}$bserve good faith and justice

towards all nations.

Cultivate peace and harmony within.

———————————

George Washington, 1732–1799

PRESIDENT OF THE UNITED STATES OF AMERICA

There is enough in the world

for everyone to have plenty

to live on happily and to be

at peace with his neighbors.

———————————

Harry S. Truman, 1884–1972

PRESIDENT OF THE UNITED STATES OF AMERICA

We cannot learn from one another until we stop shouting at one another — until we speak quietly enough so that our words can be heard as well as our voices.

———————

Richard M. Nixon, 1913–1994

PRESIDENT OF THE UNITED STATES OF AMERICA

*There can never be peace
between nations until first there is
the true peace which is within
the souls of men.*

Elizabeth Kübler Ross, b. 1926

SWISS-BORN AMERICAN PSYCHIATRIST AND WRITER

Observe good faith and justice
towards all nations.
Cultivate peace and harmony
with all.

George Washington, 1732–1799

PRESIDENT OF THE UNITED STATES OF AMERICA

THE VOICE WITHIN

$\mathcal{I}$ desire to so conduct the affairs of

this administration that if at the end,

when I come to lay down the reins of power,

I have lost every other friend on earth,

I shall at least have one friend left,

and that friend shall be down inside of me.

———————

Abraham Lincoln, 1809–1865

PRESIDENT OF THE UNITED STATES OF AMERICA

$\mathcal{T}$he one thing that doesn't

abide by majority rule

is a person's conscience.

―――――――

Harper Lee, b. 1926

AMERICAN NOVELIST

He that loses his conscience

has nothing left worth keeping.

———————

Isaak Walton, 1593–1683

ENGLISH WRITER

What is moral

is what you feel good after,

and what is immoral

is what you feel bad after.

———————————

Ernest Hemingway, 1899–1964

AMERICAN NOVELIST

K*eep pace with the drummer you hear,*

however measured or far away.

———————————

Henry David Thoreau, 1817–1862

AMERICAN ESSAYIST AND POET

The voice of conscience is so delicate that it is easy to stifle it; but it is also so clear that it is impossible to mistake it.

———————

Anne de Stael, 1766–1817

SWISS-BORN FRENCH WRITER

A *peace above all earthly dignities,*

A still and quiet conscience.

William Shakespeare, 1564–1616

ENGLISH PLAYWRIGHT AND POET

BLESSINGS AND PRAYERS

Deep peace of the running wave to you.

Deep peace of the flowing air to you.

Deep peace of the quiet earth to you.

Deep peace of the Son of Peace to you.

———————

Celtic benediction

The peace of God, the peace of men,

Be upon each window, each door,

Upon each hole that lets in light,

Upon the four corners of my house,

Upon the four corners of my bed.

———————

Gaelic blessing

O God,

help us not to despise or oppose

what we do not understand.

William Penn, 1644–1718

ENGLISH QUAKER AND FOUNDER OF PENNSYLVANIA, USA

$\mathcal{L}$et there be many windows in your soul,

That all the glories of the universe

May beautify it.

———————

Ralph Waldo Trine, 1866–1958

AMERICAN POET AND WRITER

N*ow may every living thing,*

young or old, weak or strong,

living near or far, known or unknown,

living, departed or yet unborn,

may every living thing be full of bliss.

———————

Buddha, c.653–483 BC

INDIAN RELIGIOUS TEACHER, FOUNDER OF BUDDHISM

$\mathcal{R}$eflect on your present blessings,

of which every man has many,

not on your past misfortunes,

of which all men have some.

———————————

Charles Dickens, 1812–1870

ENGLISH WRITER

Bless the four corners of this little house

And be the lintel blessed;

And bless the hearth, and bless the board

And bless each place of rest.

———————————

Traditional English blessing

Let nothing disturb you.

Let nothing frighten you.

Everything passes away

except God.

———————

St Theresa, 1515–1582

SPANISH NUN

Let me be a little kinder,

Let me be a little blinder

To the faults of those around me.

Edgar A. Guest, 1881–1989

ENGLISH-BORN AMERICAN JOURNALIST, POET AND WRITER

$\mathcal{G}$od Grant me

the serenity to accept the

things that I cannot change,

The courage to change the

things that I can,

And the wisdom to distinguish

the one from the other.

———————

Reinhold Niebuhr, 1892–1971

AMERICAN THEOLOGIAN

May you have food and raiment,

A soft pillow for your head.

May you be half an hour in heaven

Before the devil knows you're dead.

———

Celtic blessing

WORDS

OF

WISDOM

*K*eep me away from the
wisdom which does not cry,
the philosophy which does not laugh
and the greatness which does not
bow down before children.

———————

Kahlil Gibran, 1883–1931

LEBANESE POET, WRITER AND MYSTIC

W*e act as though comfort and luxury*

were the chief requirements of life,

when all that we need to make us

really happy is something to be

enthusiastic about.

———————————

Charles Kingsley, 1819–1875

ENGLISH WRITER AND CLERGYMAN

If you achieve success,

you will get applause, and

if you get applause you will hear it.

My advice to you

concerning applause is this:

enjoy it but never quite believe it.

———————————

Robert Montgomery, 1807–1855

ENGLISH PREACHER AND POET

As you grow older,

I think you need to put your arms

around each other more.

———————

Barbara Bush, b. 1925

FIRST LADY OF THE UNITED STATES OF AMERICA

The perfume of sandalwood,

the scent of the bay leaf and jasmine,

travel only as far as the wind.

But the fragrance of goodness travels

with us through all the worlds.

Like garlands woven from flowers,

fashion your life as a garland of

beautiful deeds.

———————————

Buddha, c. 563–483 BC

INDIAN RELIGIOUS LEADER AND FOUNDER OF BUDDHISM

I do not believe that sheer suffering teaches. If suffering alone taught, all the world would be wise, since everyone suffers. To suffering must be added mourning, understanding, patience, love, openness and the willingness to remain vulnerable.

Anne Morrow Lindbergh, 1906–2001
AMERICAN PILOT, POET AND WRITER

$\mathcal{G}$o forth into the busy world and love it.
Interest yourself in life, mingle kindly with
its joys and sorrows, try what you can do for
others rather than what you can make them
do for you, and you will know what it is
to have friends.

Ralph Waldo Emerson, 1805–1882

AMERICAN ESSAYIST AND POET

To have reason

to get up in the morning,

it is necessary to possess

a guiding principle.

A belief of some kind.

A bumper sticker, if you will.

———

Judith Guest, b. 1936

AMERICAN NOVELIST

E*xpect trouble as an inevitable part of life,*

and when it comes, hold your head high,

look it squarely in the eye and say,

'I will be bigger than you.

You cannot defeat me.';

then repeat to yourself

the most comforting words of all,

'This too will pass.'

———————

Ann Landers, b. 1918

AMERICAN ADVICE COLUMNIST

Even at the worst there is a way out,

a hidden secret than can turn failure into

success and despair into happiness.

No situation is so dark that there is not

a ray of light.

———————————

Norman Vincent Peale, 1898–1993

AMERICAN WRITER AND MINISTER

One should treat oneself as one does one's friends – critically but with affection.

Frances Partridge, b. 1901

DIARIST AND LAST OF THE BLOOMSBURY SET

$\mathcal{K}$eep away from people who try
to belittle your ambitions.
Small people always do that,
but the really great make you feel
that you, too, can become great.

———————

Mark Twain, 1835–1910

AMERICAN WRITER

If we make our goal to live a life of compassion and unconditional love, then the world will indeed become a garden where all kinds of flowers can bloom and grow.

———————

Elisabeth Kübler-Ross, b. 1926

SWISS-BORN AMERICAN PSYCHIATRIST AND WRITER

$\mathcal{T}$o be content,

look backward on those

who possess less than yourself,

not forward to those

who possess more.

———————

Benjamin Franklin, 1706–1790

AMERICAN STATESMAN AND SCIENTIST

T reat people as if they were what
they ought to be, and you can
help them become what they are
capable of becoming.

Johann von Goethe, 1749–1832

GERMAN POET, WRITER AND SCIENTIST

B*y compassion,*

we make others' misery our own,

and so, by relieving them,

we relieve ourselves also.

———————————

Thomas Browne, 1605–1682

ENGLISH AUTHOR AND PHYSICIAN

You gain strength, courage and

confidence by every experience in which

you really stop to look fear in the face.

You must do the thing you cannot do.

———————

Eleanor Roosevelt, 1884–1962

FIRST LADY OF THE UNITED STATES OF AMERICA

$\mathcal{W}$hen we do the best we can,

we never know what miracle is wrought

in our life or the life of another.

Helen Keller, 1880–1968

AMERICAN WRITER AND LECTURER

You know,

by the time you've reached my age

you've made plenty of mistakes

if you've lived your life properly.

———————

Ronald Reagan, b. 1911

PRESIDENT OF THE UNITED STATES OF AMERICA

I think these difficult times have helped me to understand better than before how infinitely rich and beautiful life is in every way and that so many things that one goes around worrying about are of no importance whatsoever.

Isak Dinesen (Karen Blixen), 1885–1962

DANISH WRITER

If there were nothing wrong in the world, there wouldn't be anything for us to do.

George Bernard Shaw, 1856–1950

IRISH DRAMATIST, WRITER AND CRITIC